3 1082 07632 9716

DAMAGE NOTED BEFORE CHECKOUT

SOME CRAYON RESIDUE

DATE 9/10/19 INITIALS RK

ALPK04

DEMCO

ANIMALS

Butterflies

by Kevin J. Holmes

Content Consultant:
Gary A. Dunn
Director of Education
Young Entomologists' Society

Bridgestone Books
an imprint of Capstone Press

Bridgestone Books are published by Capstone Press
818 North Willow Street, Mankato, Minnesota 56001
http://www.capstone-press.com

Library of Congress Cataloging-in-Publication Data
Holmes, Kevin J.
    Butterflies/by Kevin J. Holmes.
    p. cm.--(Animals)
    Includes bibliographical references (p. 23) and index.
    Summary: An introduction to butterflies' physical characteristics, habits, behavior, and
relationships to humans.
    ISBN 1-56065-743-X
    1. Butterflies--Juvenile literature. [1. Butterflies.] I. Title.
II. Series: Holmes, Kevin J. Animals.
QL544.2.H65   1998
595.78'9--dc21

                                                    97-31855
                                                      CIP
                                                       AC

Editorial Credits
Editor, Martha E. Hillman; cover design, Timothy Halldin; photo research, Michelle L. Norstad
Photo Credits
Dembinsky Photo Assoc. Inc./Adam Jones, 6
GeoIMAGERY/Jan W. Jorolan, 4
Dan Polin, 12
Root Resources/Jim Flynn, 18
James P. Rowan, 14, 16
Unicorn Stock Photos/H. Schmeiser, cover; Ron Holt, 8; Jeff Greenberg, 20
Michael Worthy, 10

Table of Contents

Fast Facts

Kinds: There are between 15,000 and 20,000 kinds of butterflies in the world.

Range: Butterflies live everywhere on earth except Antarctica.

Habitat: Butterflies live among trees, plants, and flowers.

Food: Caterpillars eat leaves, grass, flowers, and weeds. Adult butterflies drink nectar from flowers. Nectar is a sweet liquid in flowers.

Mating: Some butterflies can mate at any time. Many mate in the spring and summer.

Young: Newborn butterflies are caterpillars. They hatch from eggs. Caterpillars turn into chrysalises. Chrysalises change into butterflies.

Butterflies

Butterflies are insects. An insect is a small animal with a hard outer shell. Insects do not have a backbone. All insects have six legs. Their bodies have three parts. Most insects have wings.

Some butterflies look like moths. But moths and butterflies are different. Most moths fly at night. Butterflies fly during the day. Most moths have hairy bodies. Most butterflies have little hair.

Some butterflies live for only a few days. Others live for a few months. A few kinds of butterflies live up to five years. Butterflies that live in warm places live longer.

There are between 15,000 and 20,000 kinds of butterflies. Butterflies live everywhere in the world except Antarctica.

Butterflies live everywhere in the world except Antarctica.

Life Stages

Butterflies go through four life stages. The first stage is the egg stage. Some female butterflies lay a few eggs. Others lay as many as 1,500 eggs.

Larvas are butterflies in the second life stage. Larvas hatch from eggs. Butterfly larvas are also called caterpillars.

Caterpillars molt several times as they grow. Molt means to shed a layer of skin. Caterpillars molt into pupas.

Pupas are butterflies in the third life stage. Butterfly pupas are called chrysalises. Chrysalises have shells around them. They change into adult butterflies.

The fourth life stage is the adult stage. The shells of chrysalises crack. Adult butterflies come out. Their wings are wet. The butterflies hang upside down until their wings dry. Then they fly away.

Caterpillars and chrysalises are two butterfly life stages.

Appearance

Butterflies have small bodies with large wings. Their wings can have many colorful patterns.

A butterfly's body has three parts. The front part is the head. The head of a butterfly holds a pair of antennas. Butterflies use antennas to smell and feel. The head also holds a proboscis and two eyes. A proboscis is a tongue shaped like a tube.

The middle part of the butterfly is the thorax. Four wings grow out of the thorax. Three pairs of legs are on the thorax. The thorax also has some spiracles. Spiracles are tiny holes that butterflies use for breathing.

The back part of a butterfly is the abdomen. The stomach is in the abdomen. More spiracles are on the abdomen.

Butterfly wings can have many colorful patterns.

Homes

Most butterflies live near flowers. All butterflies depend on plants. They find their food in trees, flowers, grasses, and weeds. Butterflies also hide in plants.

Some butterflies live in deserts. Plants do not grow when deserts are dry. Desert chrysalises may enter diapause for up to five years. Diapause is a period of rest. Chrysalises wait until rain falls. Then they come out as adult butterflies.

Some butterflies live in places that have cold winters. Some spend the winter in the chrysalis stage. Some adult butterflies enter diapause during the winter. They rest in trees or plants.

Most butterflies live near flowers.

Food

Butterflies eat different foods during each life stage. Caterpillars eat a lot to prepare for the next life stage.

First, caterpillars chew out of their egg shells. They eat the shells. Then they eat plants around them. Caterpillars eat leaves, grass, flowers, and weeds. Some even eat other insects.

Butterfly chrysalises do not eat. They live off the food they ate as caterpillars.

Adult butterflies drink instead of eating. They cannot chew food. Adult butterflies can only drink through their proboscises.

Butterflies fly from one flower to another. They drink nectar from flowers. Nectar is a sweet liquid in flowers. Some butterflies also drink juices from fruit.

Butterflies drink nectar from flowers.

Enemies

Butterflies have different enemies during each life stage. Birds, lizards, and other animals eat caterpillars. Some caterpillars are poisonous. They are brightly colored. Their colors warn other animals not to eat them. These caterpillars often eat poisonous plants.

Some caterpillars use camouflage to stay safe. Camouflage is coloring that makes an animal look like its surroundings. Camouflaged caterpillars are hard for enemies to see.

Camouflage helps chrysalises, too. Some chrysalises look like dead leaves, berries, or dirt.

Birds, spiders, and frogs eat adult butterflies. Toads, lizards, and mice also eat butterflies. Sometimes butterflies fly away to stay safe.

Many butterflies' wings are camouflaged. This keeps them safe when they are not flying. Their colors match the plants they rest on.

Many butterflies' wings are camouflaged.

Monarch Butterflies

Monarch butterflies are easy to spot. Their wings are dark orange with black lines and white spots.

There are more than 300 kinds of monarchs in the world. Most kinds of monarchs live in Asia. Four kinds of monarchs live in North America.

Many monarchs migrate in the fall. Migrate means to move from one place to another.

North American monarch butterflies fly south for the winter every year. They migrate from Canada and the United States to Mexico. Monarch butterflies often migrate in large groups. Several million monarchs may gather in one place after migrating.

North American monarchs fly north in the spring. Many stop along the way to mate and to lay eggs. Mate means to join together to produce young.

Many monarch butterflies migrate in large groups.

Butterflies and People

Butterflies help people by pollinating plants. Pollinate means to carry pollen from one flower to another. Pollen is tiny grains that flowers produce.

Pollen helps flowers make seeds that become new plants. Some of the flowers are on fruit trees. Pollen helps flowers turn into fruit. People eat the fruit from these trees.

Pollen sticks to the bodies of butterflies. Butterflies spread pollen by flying from flower to flower. Many plants need butterflies to pollinate them.

Sometimes people hurt butterflies. They put poisons on plants to keep harmful insects away. Some of these poisons hurt butterflies, too.

People can help butterflies. They can plant flowers and trees. They can put fewer poisons on plants. People can make safe places for butterflies to live.

People can help butterflies.

Hands On: Make a Butterfly

Many butterflies are colorful. You can make a butterfly.

What You Need

Crayons	Wax paper	Wooden clothespin
Sharpener	Pipe cleaners	Iron Scissors

What You Do

1. Ask an adult to help you.
2. Sharpen the crayons. Gather the shavings.
3. Cut the wax paper into two squares. Both squares should be the same size.
4. Arrange the shavings on one piece of wax paper. Cover this square with the other square.
5. Ask the adult to iron the wax paper until the crayon shavings melt. The adult should set the iron on low heat.
6. After the wax paper cools, the two pieces will stick together. Cut them into the shape of a heart.
7. Stick the clothespin over the middle of the heart. This is your butterfly's body.
8. Twist the middle of the pipe cleaner around the top of the clothespin. It should look like two antennas. Now you have your own colorful butterfly.

Words to Know

caterpillar (KAT-ur-pil-ur)—the second life stage of a butterfly

chrysalis (KRISS-uh-liss)—the third life stage of a butterfly

diapause (DYE-uh-pawz)—a period of rest

insect (IN-sekt)—a small animal with a hard outer shell and six legs; an insect's body has three parts.

mate (MATE)—to join together to produce young

migrate (MYE-grate)—to move from one place to another

nectar (NEK-tur)—a sweet liquid in flowers

proboscis (pro-BOS-kiss)—a tongue shaped like a tube

spiracles (SPIHR-uh-kuhls)—tiny holes a butterfly uses for breathing

Read More

Owen, Oliver S. *Caterpillar to Butterfly*. Edina, Minn.: Abdo & Daughters, 1994.

Pringle, Laurence. *An Extraordinary Life*. New York: Orchard Books, 1997.

**Butterfly Lovers
  International**
210 Columbus Avenue
San Francisco, CA 94133

**Young Entomologists'
  Society**
1915 Peggy Place
Lansing, MI 48910-2553

Butterfly World
http://www.introweb.com/butterfly/

Children's Butterfly Site
http://www.mesc.nbs.gov/butterfly.html

Monarch Watch
http://www.MonarchWatch.org/